COUNTRY OF GHOST

COUNTRY OF GHOST

POEMS

Gaylord Brewer

RED HEN PRESS | Pasadena, CA

Book layout by Michelle Olaya-Marquez

Author photo by Trevor Amery

Library of Congress Cataloging-in-Publication Data

Brewer, Gaylord, 1965–

  [Poems. Selections]

  Country of ghost : poems / Gaylord Brewer.—First edition.

    pages ; cm

  ISBN 978-1-59709-313-2 (softcover)

  I. Title.

  PS3552.R4174A6 2015

  811'.54—dc23

                        2014037130

The National Endowment for the Arts, the Los Angeles County Arts Commission, the Dwight Stuart Youth Fund, the Los Angeles Department of Cultural Affairs, the Pasadena Arts & Culture Commission and the City of Pasadena Cultural Affairs Division, Sony Pictures Entertainment, and the Ahmanson Foundation partially support Red Hen Press.

First Edition

Published by Red Hen Press

www.redhen.org

ACKNOWLEDGMENTS

These poems were written during a trilogy of summer residencies: in 2009 at Can Serrat, in the village of El Bruc outside of Barcelona; in 2011 at the Arteles Arts Center in rural Finland; and in 2012 at the Camac Centre d'Art, on the Seine an hour from Paris. Ghost's appearance on the first two trips startled me, but by the time I got to France I was half-expecting him. Although he hounded me (or, he might argue, vice versa) across Europe for four years, he never appeared at the house in Tennessee. I believe I understand the reasons for this, and I am, I believe, grateful for his restraint. A wish for my haunting and haunted friend: I'm not certain what happened in that small church, its door inexplicably open in the dark. But I hope you found some peace. Perhaps we will meet again.

Vis-à-vis the three residencies: Thanks to my tolerant and forgiving hosts and to the whole gang of misfits, outlaws, and co-conspirators, first wave to last. You know who you are and you know I saw it happen.

My appreciation to Middle Tennessee State University for a Faculty Research and Creative Activity Committee grant that enabled the completion of this manuscript.

Section One, now entitled "Spain: Ghost Born," was published as the chapbook *Ghost*, winner of the 2010 Anabiosis Press Chapbook Contest. A grateful nod to Richard Smyth for the vote of confidence.

Thanks, finally, to the editors of the following journals: *Amoskeag,* "Ghost Cleans Himself Up Before Visiting the Monument of the War Dead"; *Asheville Poetry Review,* "Following a Dream of Apocalypse, Ghost Appreciates the Beauty of the Dead and the Day," "Ghost Practices His Funeral," "Ghost Takes a Sunday Swim in the Lake"; *Bayou,* "Ghost Cleans Himself Up Before Visiting the Monument of the War Dead"; *Birmingham Poetry Review,* "After Contemplating the Nature

of Time, Ghost Steps from His Room into Sunlight," "Ghost, Revenant,"
"Ghost Says Goodbye," "On the Night Bus Again, Ghost Is Startled by His Own
Reflection"; *Briar Cliff Review,* "Ghost Considers the Altered Nature of His Sleep
and a Consummation to Be Wished," "Ghost Writes a Postcard to His Wife"; *The
Cape Rock,* "Ghost Takes the Evening Bus, Briefly Dozes"; *The Chattahoochee
Review,* "After Ascending to the Black Virgin, Ghost Attempts a Telephone Call,"
"Ghost Bleeds," "Overcome by a Mild Despair, Ghost Attempts and Fails to Leave
His Room"; *The Evansville Review,* "Becoming Ghost," "Ghost Visits the Cemetery
of Virrat, Composes a Letter to His Dearest Friend," "On Summer Solstice, Ghost
Listens to the Wind's Message"; *Hawai'i Review,* "Ghost as Housekeeper"; *Kestrel,*
"Ghost Faces Another Tuesday Morning"; *The Louisville Review,* "Ghost Attends
the Midnight Sun Festival as a Special Guest," "Ghost Begins His Consultation with
the Next River"; *Nashville Arts Magazine,* "Ghost Writes a Postcard to His Wife";
Number One, "Ghost Awakens Groggily, Considers the Nature of Consciousness,
Et Cetera," "Ghost, Invited to Sauna, Indulges the Obvious Analogies," "Ghost
Visits the Quay in Tampere, Eats Blood Sausage," "On the Pier, Ghost Finds a Love
Note, Paper of Seeds, and Accepts Its Invitation," "A Rainy Day and Monday for
Ghost"; *Pinyon,* "Ghost Reconsiders the Romance of the Piano Player"; *Poem,*
"At 3:00 a.m., Ghost Tries and Fails Not to Recollect His Wedding Day," "Ghost
Addresses the Virgin with a Fond Farewell," "Ghost Considers a Dive from the
Loft of His Monastic Chamber," "Ghost Shares a Moment with Orangutan,"
"Ghost Waits"; *A Poetry Congeries,* "Following Three Years of Wandering, Ghost
Breaks His Silence with the Virgin," "On Mother's Day, Ghost Walks the Road
to Courtevant, Closed by Flood, and Collects a Simple Bouquet," "Playing Fetch
with the Local Dog, Ghost Recalls a Photograph"; *Prairie Schooner,* "After Three
Days, Ghost's Fever Breaks," "At the Plaça del Rei, Ghost Acknowledges One of
His Own," "Awaking from Nightmares, Ghost Hangs His Laundry"; *River Styx,*
"Ghost Reveals a Back-to-Basics Platform to His Constituency"; *Skylight* (Ireland),
"Ghost Reveals a Back-to-Basics Platform to His Constituency"; *Smartish Pace,*

"Ghost Awakes with a Hangover, Assigns Away His Last Earthly Possessions," "Ghost Holds His Vow of Fasting for Nearly Twelve Hours," "Ghost Visits the Coves Salnitre," "Trimming His Nails, Ghost Makes a Foreboding Discovery"; *Sugar House Review*, "Behind the Artificial Night of His Curtain, Ghost Is Assaulted by a Single Fly," "Following a Visitation by Death and the Virgin, Ghost Dreams of His Dogs," "Ghost Dreams of the Last Time He Held His Father."

CONTENTS

France: Ghost Passage

COUNTRY OF GHOST

But no one among them thought that anyone could raise the
dead. It had occurred to no one. Most of them believed, or so I
learned, that it should not even be tried, that it would represent
a mockery of the sky itself. They felt, as I felt, as I still feel, that
no one should tamper with the fullness that is death. Death
needs time and silence. The dead must be left alone with their
new gift or their new freedom from affliction.

—Colm Tóibín,
The Testament of Mary

She says, I don't know you
like I used to know you,
something's changing these days.
She says, I almost hate to say it,
but I liked you better the old way.

And I say, baby, I'm just fading,
watch me fading away.
'Cause get it right or wrong,
sooner or later, we all get gone.

—Nathan Bell, "We All Get Gone
(Gaylord Brewer's Traveling Blues),"
from the album *Black Crow Blue*

SPAIN: GHOST BORN

BECOMING GHOST

As you withdraw from the beloved ones,
first in mind, then abused beast of the body
following, you will find speech no longer
plausible. Suggestive turns of hip or shoulder

suffice. The night as long surmised
requires no further recompense. The sweat
of your face, your wetted hair no more
than a fevered baptism of exchange.

Fly, wraith. Your secrets mean nothing
to anyone now. Fly to a moon-washed city
of dust and stone. To the cemetery
locked to you, the church undiscovered,

shuttered houses murmuring as you pass.
Ghost breathes on for awhile, sorry nostalgia—
so breathe. If the heart still struggles,
you may share too that fading urgency.

Where were you going? Where you have
arrived, of course. Recognize this place
and, perhaps, weep or smile at the knowledge
you pursued. The loneliness found instead,

its barbarism and solace. There, seeker—
crevasse, mountain, flickering shore.
Dark turn of wing. The bridge where you
pause, a last bittersweet time, as you cross.

GHOST CONSIDERS A DIVE FROM THE LOFT OF HIS MONASTIC CHAMBER

Your head grazes centuries-old beam
as cold toes clench edge of planking.
Can ghouls commit suicide? You'd never
have thought so, but so much has had to be
forgotten. Anyway, you're joking around,

flirting with the rush. The height's
only enough to hurt. A crumbled arch
of brick, twenty-foot sheer shroud of curtain
frame your solitary bed, wool blanket
and sleepless pillow. Inventory of penance—

low door scarred raw inside, bolted out.
Distorted mirror, voiceless, as if reflecting
a body under water. Enduring sandals.
Overturned can of talc to ease odor and chafe.
Ghost is only human. And, ironic tempt

by your host, a cockeyed chandelier
you wouldn't want to swing from. Stair
so rickety-narrow it may grant your wish
some night whether you wish or not.
Arms stretched wide, hung in airy shadow,

you can nearly touch each enclosing wall
of torn plaster. To stand straight again,
ever leave this peaceful, purgatorial tomb,
you'll need a safe means of descent.
Yes, one way or the other a leap of faith.

GHOST ADDRESSES THE VIRGIN
WITH A FOND FAREWELL

Averted glance neither come-on nor dismissal—
a tease. Literally, she sees right through your kind.
You've come to enjoy her unerring profile,
girlish lips, gold gilt of modest shawl. Her halo

crooked antenna of another world.
What scores, songs, holy static she receives.
She's a good listener, doesn't mind staring,
even caress of shoulder. And not the cold bargain

you'd expect. Warm, polished from the wood.
Fate, chance, or nothing at all delivered you
to her detailed bust, bolted in place—as not to fall
or be spirited away, rude protection nonetheless—

to a recess of wall washed a child's blue.
Even a brute such as *toi* has appreciated stillness,
studied common quiet, tithed hours
aping her placid certainty. This grotto getaway.

Three days now, your time together finished.
A marriage of sorts? Fingers trace glowing cheek,
smooth neck. She gets in a ghost's head.
Goodbye, dear Mary. Put in a fair word for me.

GHOST TAKES THE EVENING BUS, BRIEFLY DOZES

You nod, nod, as if forgiving
subdued rows of voices,
so earnest. You intuit each phrase

though words are nonsense.
The flash of next nameless village.
Force eyes open. Doors yawn—

one old woman, clawing sweater
and bag, shuffles for her alley.
Then it's mountains again,

deepening bruise of sky.
Today discarded, engine narcotic
hum of disappointed night.

You work the crowd, seat to seat,
lap to lap, so exquisitely exhausted
you're sure of truth in each

cautious face, meager life—
you're in the boat too, Ghost—
rolling on to darkness, coin

exchanged, lunatic at the wheel.
Why speak of dignity this time
of day? Another village, other boy

squinting startled, suspicious.
Glowing windows pass him by.
Your head, heavy stone, drops.

Next stop, perhaps one after,
that's yours. Don't worry—you'll
surely know it when you see it.

AFTER CONTEMPLATING THE NATURE OF TIME,
GHOST STEPS FROM HIS ROOM INTO SUNLIGHT

Neither eternal metronome nor, quite, infinite
stream, still you hear the endless tick-tock
in the head, no quitting it. Between heartbeat
of seconds, a hundred, a thousand,
ten thousand others, small impeccable trilling,
the whirr, hum, quiet ceaseless roar
announcing was and wasn't, will and won't be.

Something like that. Anyway, no ignoring
for one moment. Beyond shuttered windows
the bus pulls away, the laughing assurances,
farewells, tires on gravel and a relative
calm restored. Time in the ache of hinge
opening, time in the fanfare of leaves,
time in the grooved joints of wrist and ankle.

Outside this room, day follows night,
or night day, as you will, cold certainty
that almost convinces. You wait for no one
at no appointment, and right on time no one's there.
Count the clock in the noggin. Count the luck.

You raise yourself from a single sheet,
push forward through doors and passage.
Blink: It is noon. It is midnight. It is dawn.
Light hot on your skin. The wood pigeon,
plumped and gray, wild from the branch.
A body looks up, signifies your existence still.
Even Ghost can use a little company.

GHOST HOLDS HIS VOW OF FASTING
FOR NEARLY TWELVE HOURS

You really believed the interim life meant
no more diets, lean body and sated appetite?
Now conviction muttered to night birds,
to attain faster some realm of pure spirit.
Resolve held, too, until sunlight angled

a carving knife through afternoon window
and the cling clang of the bell was real,
not children playing at noise. Ethereally quick
to table, past the skinny young man
clumsy at the meat platter. Joint crack,

quick serrated edge, thieved shank
free in your hand. Ghost at the head of the meal—
blessing potatoes lathered in gravy fat,
crossing with a fistful of the lamb of Christ
—whatever—all over your sticky smile.

This is Holy Day, Fête, glass of wine raised
to animal heaven in blood communion.
Greasy mortality and the well-gnawed bone.
Pallid over nests of lettuce, carrot and radish,
vegetarians share nervous glances.

While silent amid a canopy of vines—
triangles of early grapes the size of nail heads—
a cat leaps, perfect, with malice to spare.
You chew on, watch him watch the others.
Future days aplenty for hunger and for want.

TRIMMING HIS NAILS, GHOST
MAKES A FOREBODING DISCOVERY

One claw at a time, each brittle, growing shell.
You chart their length almost by the hour—
every day requires attendance to manicure,
pedicure, else you curl to some grotesque facsimile
of human. But when blade slices so hungrily
through the flesh of the toe, so wide, so deep,
you can only watch mesmerized a red tide
claiming the foot, pooling across a map of tiles.

Well, why should anything surprise you?
Thin-skinned indeed. A rotted parchment barely
containing the goo. What the next delight?

Overcome by a Mild Despair, Ghost Attempts and Fails to Leave His Room

These scarred walls. Your marked hands.
All's well, Ghost, don't take the day so seriously.
Nothing was promised and little expected.

You draw on one gray sock then the other,
pull rough blanket tight across shoulders.
See, already you are on your way.

You should rise, peruse the wild garden,
give name to scent of rosemary, mint, thyme.
Lavender bloom, crumpled petal

of cistus, bush of yellow broom—touch these
and be healed. Inquire with the angel
of clay and one smiling eye, of her broken

wing, the hole in her belly a pit without a fire.
Aim straight for the week's bleak horizon.
You should leave this narrow bed

the man you were, or imagined yourself,
breathing horse breaths through flared nostrils,
fit and arrogant, laughing after a future

never assured, except one thing. Darkness
two embers in immutable fists and all the world
afraid. Silence the sun with shadow and

the stubborn chorus of one voice. Meaning—
lie back, close your eyes and wait.

AFTER THREE DAYS, GHOST'S FEVER BREAKS

Deep beneath wool coat and blanket,
heavy shirt, in the dream not a dream
you are Cristóbal Colón, malarial, fatal
last voyage to new world made old,
sea unconquered and unimpressed.
When God speaks you listen—his taunts,

the brutal puniness of your discovery.
Gradations of light in the shuttered cabin
signal day and night, ordinary trick
of time, theatre of shadow across closed eyes.
In the dream not a dream you are Christ,
wasted features stained to damp sheet,

relic for fortune hunters. Breath, heartbeat,
pulse in wounded hands and feet.
Hour, instant, distorted flash of longing—
woman's warm thigh against your own,
hand on your face, the home you left
again and again—why?—until no map

could guide you back. Hour, instant, flash—
childhood bicycle, your brother, angry,
skull of horns and the ceaseless parade,
all coffins. When you reach across the dark
for water, the table rattles, the bowl is dry.
Rebelling bones, bag of flesh, basilisk

tongue licking blood clean from lips.
Exactly now, or then, the tomb of the body
relents, just a little. Another eternity.
You sit upright, dragging an altar of rags.
Now or then, you decide to stand,
and some time or other do so. Mummy,

priest of patches, shuffle to windows.
Dare yourself to unlatch them. What day?
Sure enough, there the brick archway
of the courtyard, shattered sculptures.
A miracle of fire risen in the east, cool wind,
palms straining toward their hosannas.

GHOST AWAKES WITH A HANGOVER,
ASSIGNS AWAY HIS LAST EARTHLY POSSESSIONS

To die, be born, and die again.
What would you celebrate,
what would laughter commend?
That you're alive? Well, not quite.
How brief vows of forever,
sacrificed to tawdry morning.
But you taught the body again
to bow and obey, poured your poison
like honeyed tea. Thy will
and testament, Ghost. Speak.
Take this cup from me. It is yours.
Take these sandals and the tired dust,
this rope of leather for a belt.
Take this coat that warmed me,
these bent fingers that reached for you
and the eye that saw your beauty.
This mouth, and every word said
and unsaid to the night.

At the Plaça del Rei, Ghost Acknowledges One of His Own

The skinny boys clenched in wet t-shirts
see neither of you. Scarecrow, old graybeard,
prophet, pariah. Ghost. Little remains
but the blue fire of his eyes, steady on you.

He adjusts his box to keep ankles and bloodied
pant legs dry. The gargoyles, gleeful,
disgorge filthy torrents. You lean hard
in the archway but the slanting rain

numbs you anyway. Here, Columbus
came with bounty for his queen—rare birds,
sweet potatoes, six captive Haitians, baptized.
Tonight the square is a graveyard,

flood of five brutal and buried centuries.
The teens make a hopeless run for it.
Just you and scarecrow, his bed of cardboard
and stone. He nods, explains nothing.

When you offer the shekels from your pocket,
four dull coins, he opens a dirty hand
to take them. Then him to his journey,
you to yours, the relentless night ahead.

AFTER ASCENDING TO THE BLACK VIRGIN, GHOST ATTEMPTS A TELEPHONE CALL

I

Curiously, you hardly tire now—
last force of the body freely, fully offered.
Four hours up. Knees good, feet good,
skin expelling night toxins. Fine to be
alone, witness the world's intricate grid.
A snake—brown-striped, handsome—
suns across the path. You watch him go,
from somewhere begin a song
your father sang to you as you traveled.
Touching cheek and ear of his youngest,
nostalgic already for the moment passing,
a strange, rough reverence in his hand.
Anyway, the whole silly rhyme returns.
Claim it on the mountain as you climb.

II

Drift, Ghost, among blind flashbulbs
of the basilica, monkeys snug in a barrel,
lemmings to the sea. Boys raise a hymn
and two-step forward to mumble another day's
indecipherable blessing. Gawkers disperse.
High over the altar, the small, gleaming figure
of La Morenata, orb extended to pilgrim, saint,
sinner, whatever you bring. Her thin smile.
Dark child in her lap, His golden crown.

III

On whim, you stop at a pay phone—relic
of a gone age—punch a number long known
by heart. As they say. *When you asked she said yes—*
a miracle—and when you called your name aloud
she knew it as her own. Touch each number softly,
Ghost, as if sequence itself an invocation
of loss. Of course nobody answers. No ring,
no signal at all. Just silent distance, click
of receiver to its cradle. The long walk down.

Moving hurriedly—why?—across the city,
you disregard the cabaret, obscured
sky, glory of architecture, aroma of bread.
You taste lower lip, its warmth
and salt, and navigate alleys
toward some urgency you can't complete,

some address no longer there that never was.
Hand on cheek, where cat sliced
for her amusement—the palm's fortune
a hash of red. No surprise. You're resigned,
nearly, to this late chapter of the body's
mutilation and spoil—self-vampire, ripe

with decay, nourished and stewed
in your own dark juices. Burnt fingertips
of the hand won't heal, have split and opened
again—this the gruesome mark
Ghost leaves on all Ghost touches.
Market stalls, delivery men smoking

and loud, women skeptical of the morning's
narrative of fish and oranges.
Abandoned museums, boats tied at harbor,
statues of the embarrassed dead.
Next, university students carouse
with shirts off or swallowing frozen goodies,

expound on all that is known and all
the finery to come. You touch the side
of your nose, skin baked raw by sun.
The hand comes away dripping red. Monster,
mask your face with a cloth no longer white,
hold loneliness and shame a while.

These delirious children, laughing,
unwounded and sure, pass through.
Keep moving till you're safe again.

Obese and auburn monstrosity
of gibbous tit, sagging leather belly,
twisted straggle. Beautiful mom.
She picks a nose slit, with disinterest
eats the result, dark eyes
vague on a dream of jungle.

Or nothing. She turns
bloated profile in your direction,
child prostrate in a long arm,
its sleepy confusion, bulbous head
so finely haired to seem bald.
You think at first it's your conceit

that she watches you of hundreds
who pass each indistinct day.
No. She bends from her shelf,
fist for balance against glass,
and brings her face within inches.
You return the flat stare,

startled, anxious for its message,
press hand opposite black knuckles
in an awkward display.
She's offering something, Ghost,
but first must decide what you are.
Eyes' smothered fire, broken

wildness. For an eternity
of two minutes, three, the world's
a still axis of shared pain.
You're almost there, that close
to your lesson and place.
Then the first scream of first

human child, first maternal idiocy,
camera click. She leans slowly—
so slowly as to torture—back to her
seat and manufactured vines,
buries the baby in hairy
folds, returns her gaze to the sky.

She's gone. You never were.

AWAKING FROM NIGHTMARES,
GHOST HANGS HIS LAUNDRY

Horrible, most horrible, and common.
Crimes of your own conception
against all, it seems, who dared love you,

scenes that can't die quickly enough
in the irradiating day. It didn't happen,
or not much, or that you recall, so why

the net of horrors dredged nightly?
Were you such, or feared or longed
to be? Untangling the knot of garment helps.

Sunlight warm on morning, wrens
and sparrows to their work, damp grass.
Threadbare socks just so, each according

to design and matching other.
Hung pants collapsed and amputated.
Best the shirts. Empty, reaching arms,

the stitching worn, yes. But dark cloth—
fabric spun from earth and worm—enrobing
air, burned lighter each moment,

gentle sail to all held and released,
insinuation of the body that was Ghost,
its terrors and longings. Then nothing.

GHOST VISITS THE COVES SALNITRE

Count ragged cadence: two hundred forty-four
steps up the mountain. Another Sunday,
parody of ascent. You're a stinking mess
by the time you reach the hole, nod last look

at lives on the surface, and step across.
Cold-dark slap, sweat immediate ice
on skin, these feel good. Enter bandit,
scholar, expelled rebel. Earth opens for you.

Cracked voice soars to cathedral heights,
returns in chorus. Bats long gone, smoked out
into horrible day. Claustrophobia gone too,
like everything. Just this tedious persistence.

Down Devil's Well, why not? You hold
a hand onto wet stone, the hard contours,
bring dampness to your face and kiss.
The Elephant, Wild Boar, Candelabra—

find what you will in flickering formations.
Past the Barricades, Virgin's Pavilion, awaiting
insights you expected. They never arrive.
This is no metaphor, it is the plight itself.

You try your song again. Narrowness
kills it. Raise your torch. Quick slide now
into Hell's Mouth, and that's as deep as you
may go. *Welcome, Ghost*, the mouth says. *Rest.*

ON THE NIGHT BUS AGAIN, GHOST
IS STARTLED BY HIS OWN REFLECTION

Pale blur of landscape
and the face looking back,
primitive double exposure.
How harsh, angry this phantom,
black volcanoes of eyes,
white beard, baleful visage

pretending wisdom. It's hard
to think clearly anymore.
Locked in that unforgiving
gaze, you're too weak to turn away.
The Other's got you in its sights,
mocking each nod or grimace,

doubling the signature scowl,
the sham of a lifetime's mask.
Mimicking your whole bloody story
and not much impressed.
I never want to see this bastard again.
Then the mind a blank film.

GHOST SAYS GOODBYE

Perhaps you were mistaken, too,
regarding the bridge where this began
and ends. Perhaps you may

cross again and again, then forget.
A photograph you'd avoided—
you touch its surface with what

remains of gentleness, close the drawer.
Your wife, your home, the man
you meant to be and became instead.

This morning sun blinds, hot.
There the weekly fishmonger
to visit a last time, study the oracle

of her creatures and make a choice.
Poppies above the village,
red tissue so soft it can't be felt.

A shirt, belt, sliver of soap,
a few notations and figures to tally.
And yes, if there were a ghost

of a chance for one blessing more,
deserved or otherwise—you'd pray
till the hollow body trembled.

But now a motorcar approaches,
a door closes, a voice calls out
a name you recognize was yours.

Finland: Ghost Revenant

GHOST, REVENANT

Two years passed, or twenty,
or two thousand. Your migration
strays to the edge of this gray marsh,
silent trembling of its waters.

You stand in the tatter of your
sole shirt, feet roped in same dull hide
that crossed the bridge of your origin,
vagrant without sense or decency to die.

A single black-headed gull strikes
silently against the wind. The murmur
around you neither gossip nor
greeting, just leaf, limb, and motion.

The ridge of pine and birch across
the lake, however, unbending,
jagged beneath a pale sky that refuses
the night its darkness.

So there, Ghost, is your compass.
Locate yourself in the body
and feel nothing. Drink deeply
of thought until no thought occurs.

You're just here, is all, arrived, riven,
unending. North, Ghost, north you go
until a mystery perhaps abandons,
perhaps reveals. You shall see.

GHOST DREAMS OF THE LAST TIME
HE HELD HIS FATHER

Insult to sad injury, it didn't happen,
not in that wretched place, no unseen fall
to stones and his defeated body shaking,
the senseless lips, musk of sweat and fear,

not that. Sufficient, Ghost would think,
to carry horror of the memory without
horror of the dream. A bonus of
night's bounty. Admire your blistered hands,

red flesh cratered from failed arguments
with fire. Note relentless morning arrived
and white sun risen, sky gradations of blue,
caravan of cloud, late-bloomed lavender

bowed in trite perfume. Note evidence
of damp collar on damp neck. Now bend
to that orb, ascended flame, make it burn
all loss away—real, invoked, evaded. Walk.

Ghost Awakens Groggily, Considers the Nature of Consciousness, Et Cetera

Call it sleep, if such comforts. There is no
rest to it, no renewal ever to be had.
The dreams, yes, always unforgiving,
voice of your father amused at his own
betrayed life and the heat of youth—

Hurry, son, hurry. He laughs again.
The woods around you both, somewhere,
real or imagined, as unfathomable
as the world to come. Whatever names
that floating space—sleep, trance, a word
still to discover—it claims the hours

more and more hungrily. Waking day
diminished to blur. Day and night, endless
light. Jesus, Ghost, you rhyme nonsense
and cast it as diamonds to a starless sky.
What sort of ghost is a ghost without darkness?

You're no danger except to yourself,
no fun or threat to children laughing
around their drum of fire. To mosquitoes
swarming for the last of your exhausted blood,
you're—*boo!*—hardly worth the trouble.
Leave thinking to fools and prophets. Sleep.

BEHIND THE ARTIFICIAL NIGHT OF HIS CURTAIN,
GHOST IS ASSAULTED BY A SINGLE FLY

Persistent harbinger, black and certain,
stinging kisses on ankles, wings caressing
backs of hands. It rises, rapturous, lands again
upon the meat of your bones. Quick speck
on white wall, gone before your stumbling slap.

No choice but surrender—to the gloom
of the bed you made, the vow buzzed in the ear:
In a land of light, Ghost, you arrived seeking
darkness. I am your last lover, come to share
this journey and this end. I will never leave you.

FOLLOWING A DREAM OF APOCALYPSE, GHOST
APPRECIATES THE BEAUTY OF THE DEAD AND THE DAY

Cracked shell of the city, poisoned
sky, all human agency except blood-survival
exposed in a flash. When famine calls,
the slaughter and feast. All old news to Ghost.

You stand now beside a rural lane
and watch the weary circus of the dead,
migration east as far as one can see
until the road drops. Recently they appear
without explanation. Resigned
to their trail, silent and odorless, unknowing
of the world except for a single thin face,
mouth slack and toothless, that turns
your way with what you fathom,
perhaps, as humor. Eyes lower slowly forward.
This is new, this signal to the audience.

You pass your crooked hand through
a scatter of lupine, purple cathedrals,
deeply violet blooms expanding
from bottom upward. The stinging pleasure
on your fingertips surprises. Raucous
converse of jackdaws, their wariness.
The bellies of the trees
filled with their hungry young. Your chest
fills, and breathing would be difficult, Ghost,
if breath were necessary. *Easy, easy.*
They are gone again—grim rainbow, condemned
parade, ever-extending family. You want to
follow them. You want to stay.

FOLLOWING A VISITATION BY DEATH
AND THE VIRGIN, GHOST DREAMS OF HIS DOGS

They arrive together. His hooded robe
so luminously black the room glows. Tissue
of her skin and mournful lake of eyes.
His face, shadow creased in fiery shadow.
Ghost: *Reveal the mask of the departed. Is it mine?*
Or one I loved or despised? What could have
been different? The benediction of His hand
resolves nothing. You are nailed in place,
unmoving, and her single nod, too, fails you.
You're afraid, Ghost, afraid as you've ever been.

And then you're home, home a single night
between partings, slippered in the kitchen,
gifts on table, words of love in your hand.
This brief return, bittersweet already,
startles you. Just as it does the first beast
who scents his master, yelps, leaps. Then another,
and a third, all roar and teeth now, tongue
and claw and glorious, golden fur,
a blaze of fur and fury and human laughter.
A man, a living man, amazed and laughing.

Ghost with eyes open, hair matted, skin hot.
You feel sweat on your back, behind your legs,
crawling under your body. A dark jacket
on a hook where He stood, a faded
shawl slack beside. Those fine, sweet animals,
so fair, so faithful. Were they real? Were you?
They would run howling from you now.

A RAINY DAY AND MONDAY FOR GHOST

The north folds again inside a shawl of mist,
the heat that tortured nights is vanquished.
And that concludes the thinking portion
of Ghost's day. Sit on the creaking deck
in a soft shirt. Jackdaw chicks cough and meow

in the pines, practice a first fluttering
leap at the world. They know you. Tolerance
is enough. Enough, too, to float in a nimbus
of your own silence, here where you never lived
or bore a name, to remember no one

nor to be remembered. Enough to sit stilly,
less hope or regret, until drops pricking
your wrists multiply to a cold chorus.
Lift your simple chair, cup and plate,
through the dark doorway to the room beyond.

Enough a window to look past, an edge
of slate lake, the faded hiss of a distant engine.
Enough this broken clock, its senseless knives
of hands. To stare into the unnumbered
hours of unwanting, to destroy nothing,

create nothing, all you dare ask of the day
and surely, Ghost, all you will be granted.

ON THE PIER, GHOST FINDS A LOVE NOTE, PAPER OF SEEDS, AND ACCEPTS ITS INVITATION

I love you. Plant this garden and remember.
The parched ground crumbles, ash and sand,
stones clawed to surface. But the sun, yes.
Coreopsis, Black-eyed Susan, Shasta Daisy.
Her offer lost, dismissed, discarded,

perhaps never received across the world.
Study the few words as if encrypted,
the fine texture, an illumined language
only faintly recalled. Faint, too, the perfume.
Smell it, marauder. This delicate art

not of your creation, this fateful
accident to destroy. Ghost—rend the paper
as instructed. Once, twice, a third time.
I love, reads one shape. *Love, your wife*, another.
Fragments for the earth to translate.

You press each into the trench you've dug,
then in succession a fistful of dust
until the message is fully delivered.
Coneflower, Baby's Breath, Blue Flax.
Siberian Wallflower. From the envelope

a single brown seed drops to your dirty
palm. *Columbine, Poppy.* Place it on the tongue.
Then conclude: Pour water slowly,

so not to erode such sorry work. The soil
darkens into a paste of blood. *Remember.*

Ghost always did like flowers, even on a grave.

GHOST, INVITED TO SAUNA, INDULGES THE OBVIOUS ANALOGIES

The wooden steps burn ghostly feet,
wooden seat sears ghostly ass and balls.
It's all good. A frame to the future.
You've found the darkness you sought,
one room of it, so hang your head
and fight not to howl. Your torturer

ladles water over glowing stones,
adds a second with the casual relish
of the sadist. You huddle slickly into
one another, hairy thighs grazing,
lungs bellows of fire. How much heat
can Ghost handle? Plenty. You splash

your own cup to return the favor,
take a backhand of steam in the face.
Thank you, Sir, may I have another?
Forgive me, Father, every fucking thing
I ever did and didn't do. Yes, you know
this place, where deals of men are struck.

But you're surprised—only a little,
the first time—when they parade you out
pale and inglorious under white light,
to shiver on stones in sad maleness.
Not even the stiletto of moon cares
enough to watch. She sees it all, every

night. Okay, enough cool-down
and philosophy, back to the furnace.
No worries. It only feels like eternity.

GHOST VISITS THE QUAY IN TAMPERE,
EATS BLOOD SAUSAGE

Hunger now mostly memory,
craving more of habit than belly.
But here, you dig in with the natives
at crowded tables, pierce skin
with tines designed to free the soft
black guts. Taste it, the richness

of death: blood-aroma in nostrils,
hot pudding in the mouth. Ghost food,
indeed. Across cobblestones,
stalls high with summer's first
temptings—cherries, peas in shell,
strawberries, lettuce, stalks of scallion,

small dark potatoes—their cost
writ large. What appetite you had
in your time, palette for the sweet
and the savory. Knick-knacks follow—
figurines, cups and saucers,
curled books, crocheted caps

of bright wool, dated stamps.
A lazy, roasting Friday, early June,
your last summer of the world.
Across the Tammerkoski, chimneys
of factories, brick cathedrals that mean
business and pay the devotee in cash.

Cruise boats easily tethered
to the blue. Soak it in, applaud
this city that knows no better
than to enjoy being alive. You can
stroll all morning, admire junk for sale,
weigh last coins in your pocket,

take any seat you want. Neither man
nor woman will notice. Among
the advantages, myriad, of being Ghost.

GHOST VISITS TAMPERE CATHEDRAL
TO VIEW THE FRESCOES OF SIMBERG

But first in glass, a stained reminder
of good times to come: *The pelican feeds
her young with her own heart's blood.*
Revelation, the soon end of time.
Ghost, art lover. You appreciate a nice
perversity, style that laughs as it weeps.

But for the Wounded Angel
you feel no sympathy—not for the frail
creature, wings speckled red, not for
pouty boys who bear the stretcher.
Neither helps Ghost. Better the Garden
of Death that brought you here.

Skeletons black-robed, humble, gently
tending unearthly rows of leaf and stem.
Look, Ghost: One beckons warmly
from his sockets, a pot of blue flower
held to bony breast. *The place where souls
go before entering heaven.* You would gladly

join them, no heaven required, if map
existed to this monastery of exile.
You stand a long, lingering time
under his gaze. But the altar painting,
by another, makes you frown. The dead,
restful at last, pulled decomposing

from their hole to join again the living.
You turn back to what you came for—
around the gallery's curving edge,
twelve naked boys bear a garland of roses
thicker than slim bodies. One bends
beneath the weight. One crouches toward

red bloom. Our burdened procession.
Magpie, white-plumed and low, lead us all
to thy dark wood. The trees are burning,
leaves of orange flame, and Ghost
is having a good time. Your kind of place,
ornate gloom in plaster and stone.

Hugo Simberg. 1873–1917, the text says.
Who then stares at you from the gallery,
eyes burning with a shared secret?
To whom do you nod, wink, whisper
one word of silent thanks? *Maestro.*
You got it all wrong, every exquisite detail.

AT 3:00 A.M., GHOST TRIES AND FAILS
NOT TO THINK OF HIS WEDDING DAY

Tatterdemalion, suffer that day repeated,
shade a host in black, young and old
screaming in retreat, minister
raising cross against you? Take solace,
if you will, you are not that or any man

now. Maybe none of it happened,
not that long morning of storm
and omen, dark house powerless.
Perhaps field didn't fill with kith,
blood-kin, everyone you beheld, absurdly

on cue the sun didn't tear clouds
with heat and October light. A golden
eagle circled as the service began,
though it looked like buzzard to you.
Rather to *him*, nervous groom,

but even so. Imagine that man
standing witness as his bride appeared
in dress of wild plum and moved toward
him. The man dizzy with thoughts
of her, what was ending then

and beginning, unfathomable.
After verses spoken, perhaps
he didn't lean her back, kiss her
to laughter and applause. The man
couldn't foretell how his veins

would run cold, a reptile's. Couldn't
have imagined chance after failed chance,
until no more chances. Why,
if it happened, would he think
of anything but to hold her tight

for what eternity they could steal?
But he didn't, did he? Thank God
you're not that bastard. But at 3:12 a.m.,
there are monsters then there are
monsters, if you follow Ghost's meaning.

GHOST AWAKENS EARLY,
DISTURBINGLY LIGHT OF HEART

Perhaps the problem began mid night:
roseate sky, froth of mist over field,
bellow of moose you followed into woods.
Then restful sleep: cool, scented sheet,
the senseless cinema of dream easily dismissed.

Step into morning, Ghost, in your painless body,
roadside of daisy and wild rose framed
in appreciative gaze. On the lake, white flickers
of gull. Above, islands of downy cumulus
after three days of gloom. At the shack across,
a man raises cup as if in greeting. Intolerable.

Return to your hidden spot among stone,
study the cornice's blunt cast of shadow. Sit still,
wait. Lilac bloomed out and withered
brown. Good. Black mosquitoes, numbers
refreshed by rain, mine the surface
of your welted skin, their thirst endless. Good.

And there, Ghost, when you need it most,
a gray cloud lazes toward the rest—bloated, drunk,
and huge. You stare harder at the razored
blade of shadow and light across gravel,
feel a first frisson of unrest behind the eyes
as it edges slowly, surely in your direction.

Good. Thrice. All will be well.

GHOST WAITS

But not waiting, for no desire
of arrival. Nor meditation, for no
transcendence. Unmoving on stone,

oak and spruce risen tall around you—
cage and shelter, pyre and tomb.
Grasses wreathe your thighs

with flowers of thorn, bridge
for ant and spider. It's common now:
no hours, wind not voice or touch,

sight only movement, light.
Quick cry of jackdaw punctuates
humming silence. The fiery wheel

of thought, cooled. Something takes you
or lets go. You grip down through
the crust of the earth—root ten miles

deep, spore one hundred miles wide—
to the dark, the burning core.
Those aren't the words. Neither

are bone or blood, flesh or scar,
famine or a hungering other,
distant, where you're not even Ghost.

GHOST TAKES A SUNDAY SWIM IN THE LAKE

The pinstripes of inquisitive perch
disappear as your feet stir
a bottom sponge of moss and muck.

It's cold, cold enough to get the body's
attention. You wade past lilies,
blooms erect in yellow fringe, wild

iris, cloud the situation with each
dragging step. Every action now
surfeit with meaning and no meaning.

You're up to your dripping groin,
then to the waist as you raise cup of hands
over head. Ghost the Baptist. A gull's

warning, sudden breaking shape,
gone. Otherwise just the steady
breath of afternoon across the surface.

Dive in, Ghost, a splashy, sufficient stroke
to pull you to the center, tendrils
intimate over skin. On your back,

you're more buoyant than you were alive,
arms extended, toes toward sudden sun,
dragonflies to investigate the corpse.

GHOST REHEARSES HIS FUNERAL

Leave candles unlit, the field's
bouquet unharvested, book of
scripture closed. Unbutton shirt
and trouser. There will be no visitor
for whom to robe your modesty.
Ghost, take this simple cloth

and wash the body, pale animal
marked and trembling—shoulder,
chest, thigh, calf. Wash tired feet
with care, cleansed a last time
of the roads you haunted.
Behind this curtain, the heat of day

cools. Lie now on the black down
of your bed—giving pillow,
still room, last rites of silence.
Cross hands loosely one upon
the other, where the heart lived
its urgencies and desires. There will be

no blessing for the passage, Ghost,
visitation only of your last thought—
banshee, face silhouetted, a house
on fire in the twilight. Close your eyes
with a prayer of sorts: Never again
to dream or wake.

ON SUMMER SOLSTICE, GHOST
LISTENS TO THE WIND'S MESSAGE

The birch frantic, scrub and pin oak
exhausted in their lamentations,
pine defeated and nailed in place.

The buffeted rose closes petals in submission.
The lake rushes shore and, confused,
turns back on itself. The blind sun helpless,

magpie silent. The wind hunts the woods,
teasing, clawed and cruel, its verdict
whispered for Ghost alone: *You. You. You.*

When you try to speak, it tears the sound
from your throat, a sacrifice to the sky.
Welcome to the frenzied new order of the world.

GHOST VISITS THE CEMETERY OF VIRRAT, COMPOSES A LETTER TO HIS DEAREST FRIEND

Brother, the quiet of the dead soothes,
the mute sadness of their sleep.
Why I think of you I cannot say,
nor why I cry, or for whose sake.
When did I see you? I remember boots
caked of dust, a bloodied shirt, your
smile confirming our defeat. A woman
waters the flowers of a grave, rakes
gravel in small, even rows. The tools
provided for her mark our civility.
The sky thickens to its destiny and night
comes on without solace of shelter.
Obscured in distance the docks,
the hollow, tethered boats. I cannot say
I miss you, or any of those foreign
years, or that I would care to speak
with you, touch your cheek, or relive
the testament that together we pretended
to forget. I do not wonder of your fate
or life beyond our parting, as my own
wars consume me, and night has
arrived, and my face dries in the wind.
A man approaches, places a hand on
the woman's waist. They depart together.
Only Ghost and the dead, chiseled
names and dates, shadows spreading
their ritual alms—resigned, abiding,
forgotten—these remain, and this letter
that I tear to strips and consign also
to our darkening earth.

GHOST ATTENDS THE MIDNIGHT
SUN FESTIVAL AS A SPECIAL GUEST

You sway crudely among the old
couples dancing tango in the barn,
between them. Spectral touch to his bony
shoulder, along the stick of her arm.

Indulge the mood, Ghost, celebrate
the light that never ends until it does.
Salty grilled vendace—*better than sardine,
my friend*—eaten with the fingers,

children staggering, a toast shared with
the congregated young. Flask lifted from
a pocket. You've good hands, Ghost,
claws of a sure thief. Raise it up.

Kippis: to remember and to forget.
Public words offered and the fire ascends.
House-size pyre of log, branch, needle,
flame, hungry pyramid of gold,

black smoke signaling the sky,
so hot the crowd of the living
must withdraw, cede room for this creature
that growls and eats itself.

You can't look away, face burning.
Ghost adores fire, always did. Move closer.

GHOST CONSIDERS HEAT, AND FLAME, AND THE NAME OF THE ONE WHO SPEAKS

Mercury a prick of blood
ascending, indignant of season.
The mid-day air a fist from Hell.
Don't be silly. Merely an open hand
that tightens all habit of breath

into surrender, phantom heartbeat
to arrest. A tree line begs for
the match, fate's combustible certainty.

It is yesterday, 1643, an island
in a nameless river where the witch burns—
his scream overwhelmed, his flesh
volcanic—palliative to God and man.

It is today, 1997, St. Olaf's church
an incendiary canvas, golden claw
and yellow tongue streaking their night sky.
For three days it burned as the cows
and fire trucks of Sastamala watched.

These the stale mantras you recite,
Ghost, redundancies performed
as prayer. Who speaks to you, you ask?

What voice taunts and condemns,
exhumes the lie of the earth

in taxidermy, skeleton and cinder?
You'll know the name, phantom,
as surely as you will recall your own.

And tomorrow? Charred lips, this last kiss
to the world. Ample evidence of ash
solving all that passes and all to come.

ON A LAST DAY IN FINLAND, GHOST COLLECTS A SYMBOLIC BOUQUET

The lupine that delighted
has bloomed out. Now you have
daisy and purple clover, buttercup,

solitary foxglove. This is how
life works, foolish Ghost. Admire
thorny profusion of rose,

thistle's bristled stalk.
Beast, do not rip them loose
of hold, entrail of root screaming.

Select and cut each flower
with what delicacy remains.
Two squirrels eat wild strawberries,

watch your grotesque show.
The machines have gone. The wind
is still. This, the moment, hour,

day of all that exists. Inside, a vase
of water, a hook, a coat, a blade.
Old bread discarded, a creased

photograph. Dedicate your offering
to a land you briefly touched,
that holds no knowledge of your

passing, and to these empty rooms.

GHOST VISITS THE BURIAL CAIRNS
OF SAMMALLAHDENMÄKI

The oak that shadowed cliffside, gone,
the balm of elm, of lind. Gone the enterprises
of giant and man, the pillar of churches.
Stones hold dominion, speak their weight
and silence to the lichen that abounds.

Ghost, each stone implacable and replete.
Perhaps a history of human bone remains,
a horned skull of goat, or one fragment
of bracelet, bronze burnt beyond recovery.
Perhaps a shattered bowl or scorched grains

of barley, wheat as memento. Ghastly tourist,
newly arrived, you remain. Crude rock
lifted to the light. Another, beautifully dull
and indifferent, askew to your desecrating heel.
You could stay here forever, haunting these

paths where nothing remains but what there is.

France: Ghost Passage

GHOST BEGINS HIS CONSULTATION
WITH THE NEXT RIVER

Different bridge. Same Ghost. Choose for now
not to cross. Pause at the center span, another day
dead. Always, light surrendered, bittersweet
argument of darkness. Consider your muddied way:

not ferocious in its course, but mischievous,
not mischievous but aroused, not
aroused but undaunted, eddying always
to that union with the greater voice so to lose

its own. Stand Ghost on a bridge and watch
thoughts expand, balloons loosed and popping
from his mangy head. Tonight, keep the mysteries
simple: Into the village, or out? A strange bed
for your sleep, or saturated grass of the field?

The first corpse passes beneath, face down
in the dragging current, past the mallards
you rousted from their rest. Its unresisting shape,
crooked progress, slack arms to embrace nothing

bring no surprise, only more thoughts of sleep.
You can sleep for days on end now, small eternities
of dream, or not close eyes at all. Six of one,
half dozen another. A second corpse floats into view

in the night officially commenced. Face up, swirling
as if on a weightless carnival wheel. Grinning

at Ghost or starless sky. That's enough of bridges
and bodies for now, vagaries of where, why
or why not. For now, back the way you came.

GHOST IN THE WINDOW, 2:00 A.M.

Tonight, it's you who watches the watchman.
He who claims you haunt his living world,
who tracks in fits and fury the countries
of your quest, who dismisses, returns for more.
Years blur his vision, while you, spectre,
see every nuance of the dark, an intimacy
you'd gladly relinquish. Still, a power to use.

Pity him there on a bed of blanket and stone,
turning, turning in argument with the body
to recant its aches. Thin pillow clutched
as if a raft, a fate, a clue, a fistful of memory
of a last and violent love. The metallic bell
of the church names the unholy hour—
alms for the creator, alms for the fiend.

He opens wet eyes and peers blindly
into the night, through the shadow
of Ghost amid twelve grimy stations of glass.
It is not fear in that gaze, not truth or
judgment, inquiry or challenge, but a wanting
you knew too well. Turn away, ragged one,
offer your back to this poor companion,

rich beggar, supplicant. He may follow
if he will—north into the ice or points
to be determined, but further always from
his home. Instead, the shelter of a tomb,

the heart percussive in his human chest.
Hope yet a man may live and learn.
Slim hope, even so. Ghost has been there.

BRIEF DISQUISITION UPON GHOST, WALKING, AND A VENGEFUL HEAVEN

What difference, unmoving beneath
a stone wall dissolved by five centuries
of tears, or rooted in a failed
cemetery for days, weeks, maybe decades,
yielding reed as winds precede storm,
a sigh now and again crossing torn lips?

That is, Ghost, better to hold still or
get on ye merry way, stand your ground
or endorse a fat lie of arrival?
In folklore and tale, ghouls always
stumbling ahead, refreshed from the grave,
arms an embrace of dumb hunger

for the first delicious peasant who believes
it's all a joke. So lurch along, in best
ghoulish attribute—ankles creaking, knees
decayed to pudding, hips brittle and sadistic
in soldered joints. Lurch the surface
of the ruined world. Today, the canal's

untended path, weeds the drag
that mark your limping passage. Under
a rank surface, perch breathe poison,
don't know they're dead already.
Above, Ghost, the sky darkens in welcome,
warning, wrath, or sweet indifference,

as from the small windows of the village
men read the lightning that tears
the east, signatures of fire. What of that
chill, just now, up the spine, the whispered
tremble of grass, what of a sudden,
choking dread that suffocates the space

where all their dreams had lived?

GHOST CONSIDERS THE ALTERED NATURE
OF HIS SLEEP AND A CONSUMMATION TO BE WISHED

But not sleep as you may recall suspended hours,
not dream as dream per se, pitiless collage
of exactly what you deserved—deserved or not.
Any bed a benign bed now, good enough for Ghost.
The clocks count, wind rises, again it's late.

Lay the burden of thy body down, close eyes
to a story of forgetting, what passed, what never was.
Inhale the night and its useless truth,
no harm now. Here, say, a red canvas, a staircase
descending. There, a piano in a library of babel once

revered as wisdom, the slight hands of a woman
raising a dead man's song from the keys,
lamentation and joy learned by rote. Too,
a bridge, thighs of brick and steel impassive
in the river's filthy, freezing current, body toll rising.

And there: Your wife in her soft coat, waiting
and anxious in the new snow that hides the road.
In other words, Ghost, same ole razzmatazz
of mortal coil, nightly nonsense. What else
distracts during the long darkness that has returned?

Look: She steps forward, the mark of her boots
a white trail announcing her closer, closer still.
Hair wild in her eyes and her face flush with cold.
She is smiling, she is glowing, ice bows bare limbs
where she passes and the morning light dazzles.

GHOST IN A SANGUINE MOOD

The high mid-hour of some new week
or other, nine days of rain broken,
the cock's plaintive howl. A swan holds
against the fierce current, surrenders.
The Old Man of the River hammers a staff
six times into his muddy kingdom,
calls to the wind that on the sixth day
waters will calm and blue. In sixty,
the fish will return. Thus has he visioned
and thus foretells. Believe him, Ghost,
and walk on toward a forest of birch,
careful rows planted for the purpose
of destruction. Overhead, a hidden cuckoo,
incessant, its imbecilic warning.
Pause, raise a hand to your damp face
and come away with nails painted
in blood. Blood from the eyes, from caked
mouth, by osmosis through white,
translucent skin. Blood dark,
slow and thick, turgid blood, blood whose
job is finished, seeking only escape.
Blood incantation and blood serum,
blood disease, blood cure. Blood verdict.
Ruddy, rubicund, blood cerise
the crimson fruit of spring, blood orchard
incarnadine, claret, and erubescent.
Blood rust, blood ink, blood-name on flesh.
Clotted on lips, blood distillation,
stale copper, life-exhausted, putrid-rich,

puerile. Blood bargain. Ghost, smear
claws on the stiff rag knotted at your throat,
submit to the silver invitation of leaves,
chill shadows of trees to be razed
when price and need conjoin.
A sanguinary mid-hour just tilted toward
the day's second act and body count.
Day of avian prophecy and ranting madmen.
Lick lips clean with a scorched tongue
and enjoy yourself. Good day
to be alive, or dead, or whatever.

GHOST FACES ANOTHER TUESDAY MORNING

Cloud shut evening's fiery window of heaven
and smothered the vows of the lost night.
So much for that, and morning's gray monotony.
Small birds flap and dart and scream, stupid

with energy. Coo and response of idiot doves.
Starlings patrol a bridge nobody wants to cross.
The foul waters rise though rain has ceased,
as if flood were final condition of the world,

the rule of upriver gods. A thousand eddies
chatter of calamity. A swamped boat shivers.
Even the boys who pound skinny chests, taunt
the old laws and leap curled tight and asses first,

stay away in fear. Sunday? Failed verses.
Monday? Mirage. Tuesday? All for the birds
and bird shit and rumors of ruin. Only the town
crone remains on the perilous bank, bent

and undaunted. *Marceau, Marceau* she cackles
after the dim-witted Labrador who ignores
and slobbers on, sticking gray whiskers anywhere
he shouldn't. This magnificence and more

a gift of time weighing, a chain you've no choice
but bear as unbearable, more bone-raw jewelry.
What's a ghost to do but claim and forsake it all,
endure and wait, pretend that the hour

the church bell announces exists and will pass,
then the one proceeding, extinguished to a future
other than here? What to do but enter
the ritual place moved to unmoving, no bruised

body or shackled mind, where none of this,
not even Ghost, exists or matters? And what name
may assign such a place, where a slate slab
of sky is the only salvation you will ever know?

On the Third Night of Dreams,
Ghost Slays His Slayer (a Folie à Deux)

You return to the house of your birth,
no memory. There a woman not quite
your frail mother, folded within herself
in a thin rag of gown. The near-son returns
with wounds of chest and arm,
witness to torn wrist and shoulder,
mutilated mess of a boy's body twice slain.

Hands tremble, trace laceration
of ravaging blade, rude contusion of stone.
The old hag's deaf so doesn't speak.
Her milky eye wanders. And later, hours
or moments or days, when too late,
when *he* has come again, when you have
led him to her door and the bonus of

a thin life torn away, she who didn't
quite bear you, returned with knife raised
flaring solely with your reflection, time
slowed in embrace as you lower
him to the floor, you know the weight
of his exhaustion. How little resistance,
Ghost, as you pierce soft stomach

with your shears, turn them, turn
deeper through the guts of his life.
You are close—acrid perfume of sweat,
his fading breath warm on your lips,
a sigh almost of relief, almost gratitude.

He lurches, frees pinned arm from the gore
of his back to thrust in a last faint arc

the weapon the fist contains. But it is only
an open hand, Ghost, crimson with the cost
of every lost thing, failed and damned—
a hand raised gently to your cheek.

GHOST AS HOUSEKEEPER

Bored, Ghost hit the hay early. Now
the others sleep in like the dead.
Measure flour for *la maquina pain—*
paysan, whole grain, what would
they prefer?—water, push the button.
Soon, kitchen will boast a heavenly
aroma. Brew the coffee strong
like they like it, toss a marinade
of garlic, ginger, and orange juice
for their dinner chops. Then dutifully
to the patio, collecting the butts
and trophies of night's philosophy,
wiping down the sticky plates.
Plastic, paper, glass divided for bins
and a load of towels into the wash,
voilà. Outside among blooming
cherry, dwarf pear, untie a knot
of forgotten wash—trousers, shorts,
socks, and blouse, one hard shake
and each smoothed over the line to dry
nicely in this weather. *You'll make*
someone a fine wife someday, Ghost.
Repeat the tired sarcasm as you
stand still in your favorite time of day—
quiet and alone—and hum a tune
from childhood. You're piling up
points for Hell, serving the living
with a decency they refuse themselves.
They won't even notice, of course,

lathering bread with soft, salty butter
or slipping arms into sun-warm
shirts, but *you'll* know, Ghost,
and your sponsor, The Great God Of
Everything-Nobody-Gives-A-Shit-About.
Oh, and don't forget to feed the cat,
and a bowl of cool water free of insects.
Frida rubs her plush black coat
against your ankle, licks a whisker,
groans. See? Ghost's pat on the head.

GHOST CLEANS HIMSELF UP BEFORE VISITING THE MONUMENT OF THE WAR DEAD

Hommage aux Enfants de la Commune Morts pour la France:
1914–1918—G. Simon, F. Triches, P. Hergé,
M. Ponce, J. Dauvet, M. Delaunay, J. Parisot, H. Vedel,
R. Boudin. 1939–1945—J. Dheurle, H. Robigo.

Steaming kettle, cracked bowl, palms
risen dripping to the face. The stingy foam
of a gray brick of soap rubbed hard
into jowls and chin. A stropped edge

also baptized in font—hot, hungry steel
high at attention on the cheekbone.
Ghost, study the eyes of the animal
staring back, eyes once blue and said

to be handsome, now gray, remote,
as much mystery to you as *bête noire*
as they were as man. Dead man's bowl,
by the way, dead man's soap and razor.

A casualty who won't begrudge the loan.
Bring down the militant blade, path
cleared and widened. Isthmus of upper lip.
Then from neck up—*steady, coiffeur*—

by intimate stroke, tangled prophet
transformed to quite-presentable ghoul.
Bow the head, Ghost, to a cup of hands,
dry with a rough towel left hanging

as if for your private use. For indulgence
cologne, slap of alcohol on raw skin.
The animal looks weakened, unfamiliar
to itself. But homage, Ghost, even so—

enfant-faced and en route to its grave.

GHOST REVEALS A BACK-TO-BASICS PLATFORM TO HIS CONSTITUENCY

All cemeteries shall charge a fee of entry,
collected by the mad or the infirm.
Church bells will dance in hysteria atop
each hour. All other clocks will be destroyed.

Midnight to dawn will be the Curfew of
Human Voice. Only the sleepless tide,
insomniac wind may speak, and night birds
softly over prey. For heat, the public fire

shall suffice. For reading, the pale candle.
Each supper table shall maintain two vacant
chairs, one for He Whose Name Was Stricken,
one for She Banished Forever For Her Sin.

Beside each empty plate a knife, a crust of
the day's bread, one bruised bulb of garlic.
Otherwise, all shall savor hunger equally.
At crosswalks, mongrels will hold right of way,

ceded only to the blind or the bastard child.
All shall receive salt sufficient for their wounds,
quarried from the tearful sea, parceled
each Sabbath morning when the sky confesses

storm. In winter, passports will be issued
in order of date of death. At all times, only
the Holy River shall be used for bathing, its filth
for soap, its reeds for nakedness. That is,

we must restore those values that birthed us—
no age, no gender, no color of skin, no border
to our exile, no religion save the ideology
of want. We must rise together, the living dead

too long in darkness. Together, our chorus
of wailing cannot be ignored. United, our swelled
numbers shall claim this country rightfully ours.
For barter, only the currency of our bones.

Some Diurnal Concerns for Ghost

Why will scarred hands not lie still,
Ghost, why does the phantom
heart hammer on restive and emphatic
in its cage? Why does the laughter

of children appall, their song
chill your blood, while silence
hints at some elusive peace, solitude
at promise of the restful grave?

Why does the first bloomed poppy
of the roadside, red-silk harbinger
of summer, cause only trembling?
Why would you torch every one of their

paintings, consign every canvas
to ash and nail, while this façade
of crumbled stone, mortar of patchwork
centuries, one feral vine strangling

single archway, evoke a ghostly joy?
What to divine in the shadow
fallen over another diminished day?
And inquisition, endless, what of that?

GHOST WRITES A POSTCARD TO HIS WIFE

Obverse, a landscape typical of our region,
although replace vines with genial hill
of yellow colza, full-bloomed, and replace,
if you'll permit, wheat heavy-grained
for harvest with its spring nativity,
knee-high and verdant. Replace cleared field
with ersatz lake from flood, the single
sparrow—just there—with raucous score
of black-faced gulls who know no difference.
Replace, my love, silent tractor with
plough hammered to sword on a forge
of eternal fire, the chapel with bombed-out
hotel for the touristing dead. Substitute
old man and baguette with donkey,
braying in the violence of its miction,
the crimson peony for the flowerless thorn.
Then, fair girl, we may share perhaps
one scant moment of this country to which
I have returned, one presumption of joy
or sorrow at my arrival. Indeed, replace
card itself with the errands of your day—
your sweet, living day—my faded demands
for a sorry last attempt at remedy.
With no address, no stamp, no kiss, no
signature ruined in ink, I will send this
to you, dear one, into the lost and urgent sky.

ON MOTHER'S DAY, GHOST WALKS
THE ROAD TO COURTAVANT, CLOSED BY FLOOD,
AND COLLECTS A SIMPLE BOUQUET

Of buttercups, the color she loved.
Select each stem before you tear it loose,
Ghost, a blend of flower and bud,
present and future—nothing bloomed out.

A scraggly bunch, but typical enough
of a child's thank-you for his life.
By the barbwire post, a fan of widow's
lace, then another, and a third,

for texture and for heft. Distantly,
a small red deer splashes in arcs
across the field. By the road, the shell
of one large egg, duck or swan,

brown-specked, cracked, abandoned.
A sunny Sunday afternoon in the country,
an appearance that all is well. Know
it simply: To talk with her would bless,

the woman who carried Ghost
some fifty years ago. To hear her easy
laugh, to stroll unhurried, tallying
together the fair wonders of the world.

To hold her once, before letting go
again forever, just as you unclose your fist
and commend this *bouquet sauvage*
to the river's roughly rising current.

But even if you could, you wouldn't—
not let her see her baby in this condition.
Then again, you don't blame her, either.

GHOST AS SIGNAL MASTER STANDS ON THE BALCONY
OVERLOOKING THE FERRY AND ENJOYS A SLICE OF TOAST

Who said Ghost's above a little sustaining
banality? Sometimes, you get what you need.
And what's banal, anyway, about taste
returned for one stunning moment—the chewiness

of the grain, the salt of the butter, the amber
honey of the hive? What's so common
about the spring breeze cool across bare arms,
the absolute satisfaction of nowhere to go,

no way to get there, and a bit of free-trade
commerce in the bargain? It's Woundsday,
hump day in a surrendered week already
yawning toward weekend's Fête of Nothing Special.

You lick sticky fingers clean of bee shit
and spread arms into the air, da Vinci's
perfect Ghost—the village rooster's tireless
bitching on one side, forest cuckoo's the other—

to announce it's time to Pay If You Ride.
The trains don't run and roads remain flooded.
Pilgrims crowd the bank, hands tight on tiny
pockets of coin: Fool collects the toll, Madman

oars the ferry. Ghost sips cold coffee, clangs
the bell of doom to commence the last crossing.

All aboard.

"Day One. You require no map. Shake your head
    once, pitying, at those who trace the route prescribed.
For Ghost's Way, you need only the slicing wind,
    unceasing rain as compass, latitude of your own longing.
See there: Cramped behind Rue Turenne,
    the fine Église Saint-Pantaléon, razed in the 16th century,

"again in the 18th, due to be razed again. Remark choir
    and transept, apse and nave, canopy of stone statuary
clustered about its pillars. Adjacent, the turrets
    of Hôtel de Vauluisant, now museum of the martyred
and grotesque. Marvel its crumbled façade: 'pediments,
    cartouches, cherubs, and garland.' Decadent

"syllables on the tongue, exhaled between the teeth.
    Repeat after Ghost: 'reliquaries, ossuaries.' Relics, bones.
Say the terms aloud, then forget them forever.
    Ghost Guides tell you all you need to know: Saint Pantaléon,
his hands nailed to his head in Rome in 304,
    legacy and grand achievement. Let's move on.

"Perhaps we stumble next, ravished, chilled to the soul—
    Ghost commends no restaurant, no reprieve from hunger—
upon a gallery in a cobbled lane of the *vieux cité*,
    famed for its quaint and archaic wooden structures,
rotted, infested remains of the Flood and the Fire.
    Ah, oui!, just here: An exhibition of one M. Xavier Jaliais,

"'peintre, entrée libre,' details of his 'Automorphie ou
        Principe de la Défiguration.' Remark the agonized faces,
deformity of muted screams in acrylic. But let's move on.
        Through the crowd, follow Ghost's raised skull on a pike—
throbbing legs, blistered toes, the cough in your chest,
        authenticities to which the true seeker strives—

"to the surprise that completes Day One of our odyssey:
        Behind the looming Cathédrale Saint-Pierre, we arrive at
an unremarked 10th-century square. Its history we'll ignore,
        as time is short. You're tired to death. You want your feet up.
You want that stein of beer, flute of Champagne you deserve
        and feel you've earned, to toast that you're here,

"that the others aren't. You want what you want,
        and it's of no concern to Ghost. Look, beyond an archway
no longer extant, where the Melançon no longer flows,
        there, to the slaughterhouses plying their popular trade.
Pay attention. Repeat after Ghost: 'abattoir, masacreries,
        tueries, écorcheries,' so many lovely sounds

"for the blood-and-blade trade. 'Masacreries'—
        uhmm, whisper it again and savor the mouthfeel.
You must always immerse in a country's language.
        Close your eyes. Feel the stained wooden walkway
creaking beneath tired sandals? Inhale a rancid
        perfume of grayed haunch, horse or goat,

"the gutted fowl fly-worshipped upon its hook,
    the basket of offal for a rich and hearty Sunday soup.
The holy-ghostly craftsmen of the trade
    live again in our enactment: crooked yellow smiles,
knives raised in blessèd butchery, encrusted vestments
    of apron. You must always try the local specialties.

"After a lingering menu, Ghost suggests no starred
    accommodation other than the tumult of the night,
a failed cover of archway amid the city's hidden tortures.
    As per the solitary requirement of this guide,
you are traveling alone. Attempt no conversation
    with locals, living or dead. There is no Day Two."

PLAYING FETCH WITH A LOCAL DOG, GHOST RECALLS A PHOTOGRAPH

But Dalmatian, cartoon animal, and Ghost
never a short-haired-dog kind of ghost.
Always, though, a tramp for dog enthusiasm,
being dead hasn't altered that, for love
exchanged for good scrap of fat and gristle.
Ghost stumbles forward growling, arms out,
cartoon of ghostliness, parody of the fearsome.
The stick a chewed mess of string and slobber.
You feint, lunge, assault ratty tennis ball
with stiff kick, and all parties in renewed
pursuit. When game's over—score zero-zero,
nothing-to-infinite—you massage ghostly
knuckle behind flopped ear, whisper
a few *good boy*s of support. Trace open hands
along the spotted portal of the chest,
hold briefly over perfect musculature
of taut hips. Or: Briefly in open hands
hold photo of a beautiful woman crouched
beside long-haired beast of comparable beauty,
leash slack between them. In the photo,
perhaps gravel drive is obscured already
by first felled leaves, yet the canopy
above the pair is green, too green to believe.
From the creases and smudges of peeling photo,
they smile, beautiful woman and beautiful
beast, smile at Ghost assessing behind lens.
In the photo's distance, perhaps, insinuation
of a house, glowing fragments of porch and gable
and grins aimed solely at Ghost as if in shared

and private joke, this life together too much
to believe, the slope of house overexposed
and dissolving already into dream. The photo
dissolves in your hand, a dream dissolved
to memory dissolved to wishfulness dissolved
to nothing-to-infinite. They are joyous, Ghost,
solely for you. You are part of their joy,
your care and attention are parts—not "Ghost"
of course, but a living man unseen outside
a fragile frame that can't begin to contain all
that is too much to believe. Cartoon dog chomps
rancid ball, spins, growls, challenges, waits.
Ghost stares off into great amassing clouds—
parody of the great clouds that amassed before.

FOLLOWING THREE YEARS OF WANDERING,
GHOST BREAKS HIS SILENCE WITH THE VIRGIN

Pay the Church what the Church requires,
bargain blessing for a coin echoed in silence.
Balance your purchase in open palms,
tapered, pale and—yes—ghostly. If you light
its frail rope from a last fluttering stub,

subsidize hoax of flame-to-flame, stab body
to an iron rack of nails designed for the purpose,
what might these acts portend? If unthinking
you touch fingers to the baptismal font
and raise them to your forehead, then damply

address the hem of a statue's blue gown,
and further thoughtless get stiffly to your knees
for a quiet moment, what explanation there,
or for a sudden swell of undeniable song?
The meanings, Ghost, if you'll please indulge:

One infirm light, brief and burning, to mock
the darkness that owns it. A drop of water to relieve
the traveler's fevered brow, an edge of cool stone
to dry the hands. The chorus of a whirring blade
in the street, orchestrated on the wind through seams

of colored glass. And to the oddity of Ghost bowed,
unbelieving, and painfully rising? Except the lion,
humility suits any creature—the profitable

*and pious, weary and profane. I don't buy one word
of your myth, Maria, avow one tear of your price.*

Yet here we are again. Candlelight and vows.

GHOST RECONSIDERS THE ROMANCE
OF THE PIANO PLAYER

During your life, Ghost, you longed
for the skill, cool and unannounced:
at evening's end, when *that* moment
arrived, or as surprise life-of-the-party
to those who'd known you forever,

Ghost nonchalantly on the stool, without
preamble tickling a jazzy improv
or just pounding out three blunt-force
minutes of unbridled rock'n'roll
'til you bust the damn thing or burn it.

But now, as you've surrendered
beloved *bibliothèque* where you passed
so many peaceful hours, reclined
on cushions beneath enormous beams
ancient in their silence, or touching

frayed volumes, opening a cover,
turning a yellowed page to inhale
the musk of its quiet history, as you've
surrendered these pleasures to the pasty
young man arrived without request

at the Bechstein in the window, who taps on
morning and night—a tortured Chopin;
lurching Beethoven to make you glad
for the master's deafness; worst of all
the droning tinker, tinker, tinker

of the mule at the wheel, round and round—
your only recompense, Ghost, is pride
you never took a lesson, practiced only
the muted score of the earth, only,
say, an art of listening, rather than

shitting one's endless noise into every
passing ear that didn't ask for it. Sorry,
all this racket makes a ghost testy,
who just wanted to step out of the rain
without assault of genius—blank-eyed,

slack-jawed, *idiot savant* light on the *savant*.

GHOST WEIGHS HIMSELF, BEGINS A WEEK'S DIET
IN PREPARATION FOR HIS DEATHDAY PARTY

Ghost likes a plan for failure, schedule
of sure defeat to look forward to, and likes,
too, moving the weights left and right
on the old scale, thud of the heavy marker,
then tap-tap on the lightest, forth and back

until a floating balance is achieved.
Each morning you shall rise, descend
to cellar, strip to skivvies, and step up
to the truth: How much of you remains?
What's your sorry worth by kilo and gram?

It's hard to cut back when you snack
solely of the chameleon's dish and drink
only of rain, hard to walk more
when already you pace the tombstones
till you're nearly—*ha*—dead on your feet.

But Ghost wants a lean look for the party.
Ratty hair waxed, rag and bandage rinsed
and hung dry. No gifts, please, but if
one must: a feather from the carcass
of a dove; a wild orchid torn loose by the root,

suspended dead in water; a knife for rough
carving; a brick of chalk for warnings.
And a single slice of infested cake. Okay,
two, but only a *sliver.* At Ghost's age
you really have to watch it. *Bonne fête*—

a toast to each in Hell who didn't show,
brief candle killed by rancid breath,
and the same hopeless wish as last year.

GHOST PRAYS TO DIE

Or be gone, or any end
to the clay tiles of the roofs,
the last slanting light,
the nameless birds
ceaseless in their swoop
and call, the laughter
of the living, naked
and shivering from the river.
If there be any power
to pray to for death,
take Ghost, take his tiredness,
take the unceasing
call of her unnamed voice.
Allow him pay his passage
and be gone forever,
naked in that last light
the reward of nothing,
one slanted touch of mercy,
sweet silence. No Ghost.

GHOST PAINTS A SELF-PORTRAIT AT 2:00 A.M.,
NO CRACKED MIRROR NECESSARY

From the casket, the simple materials
Ghost *peintre* requires: torn canvas
of sufficient size for an infant's shroud,
fat tubes of slate and burnt sienna—

the primaries of your palette.
And a knife for the subtleties.
Forego the cross of easel, Ghost,
spread cloth instead like a patient

upon the table—beneath a hanging
light begin. Ropy veins of severed neck.
Holes where eyes had been, smeared
in a blindfold of blood. The scraped

scream of the mouth. The roar
of white sky. Toil on, Ghost. Beyond
barred window, the river whispers
toward the city and its groaning

museums, while frogs confer on genius:
But is it any good, or even a resemblance?
Every ghoul's Picasso at 2:00 a.m. You raise
black hands, lift the ruined blade.

No human mask, that's for certain.
Finally, yes, a minor study of agony,
overwrought and taken too far.
But Ghost is Ghost's harshest critic.

On the evening when at last thirteen
    had gathered, all crowded on one long side
        of the table for posterity not of canvas
but of the river view, someone—Ghost
    in the center?—offered up the obvious quip.
        The wine that night modest but filling,

bread fresh from the baker's stone,
    the fish simply prepared with lemon and salt.
        Theologies, proposals, good laughter,
a halo of cleverness around your head.
    But you knew then, Ghost, *a thorny doubt*
        sustains the fragile rose of faith—it's better

in the Aramaic—and a truer supper to come:
    Ghost seated alone in unwashed robes
        and knotted beard, reflecting wistfully
upon return and a new kingdom's treasures.
    Tableau: Arms extended, palms open toward
        no apostle on your left, no disciple on the right.

No Peter, no John, no Bartholomew,
    no Judas, no Simon the Zealot, no servant
        boy, soldier, priest or whore—nobody.
Just a taxi spinning coffers of gravel from its
    departing tires, a gate slammed thrice in denial
        until even schemes of silver abandoned.

A sentimentalist, Ghost, you set a full table
   still, plate and gleaming knife at each place,
      goblet for the blessing. A stained pitcher,
last ragged crust of loaf, and always the river,
      stunted willows bowed weeping to its lesson.
      Black cat Mary saunters by without a look.

GHOST, HAUNTED BY THE USUAL TROPES, ENTERS THE VILLAGE CHURCH AT MIDNIGHT

Hunkered beneath the bridge, Ghost,
    you watch the red sky in the west
darken to a black and moonless possibility.
    Floodwaters recede, and again

a solitary traveler may pass the road
    if passage is desired. Crouched in stillness,
you hear a voice, distinct in Ghost's
    ear, that the church is open. The red door

approached for thirty days of Pentecôte,
    bolted thirty days, has yielded.
You do not remark this voice, question
    or name it, but unfold your creaking bones.

Why not? You've nowhere else to go.
    From deserted rooms, retrieve
by instinct a single candle, last ounces
    of wine. Beneath overstated sky,

unlit by guiding star, heaven or hunter,
    through a cackling gate that allows no
secrets, you approach the dark arch
    of stone, its mystery of eight centuries.

Enter, Ghost, with your frugal offerings—
    frail light, quaff of transfigured blood.
Take the tour you've sought: booth
    and vestment of confession, closed and hung.

Radiant dust of hymnal and pew.
  Have you been called, Ghost, or does
some careless custody enable trespass?
  It's late, you're tired, perhaps as achingly

tired as you've ever been, and prone
  to influence. Shuffle cautiously toward
shadow of altar, tapestry, crucifix,
  whatever silent immanence you seek.

That is, before a blind drop fells you, hard.
  The wine sacrificed in nails of glass,
and the candle—flame strangely risen
  for one instant—lost too to darkness.

Where are you, Ghost? I can't see you.

GHOST, GONE

Scary night noises stop.
The dog squeezes from beneath
the bed and rejoins her mother
for a snuggle. *Hello, little girl*,
the woman says aloud, and turns.
It's going to be a hot day. She needs
to get up if she intends to tend
the garden, to walk the girl
to the creek, its water so high
this month it's a small, angry river.
I miss my man!, she announces
to the room, her eyes closed.
On a morning like this, his soft shirt,
she can almost sense him next to her,
hear his breath, feel his heat.
I forgive you, she says, chokes it back.
Lord, puppy, he loved to travel.
Ha. But he always came back
to us. The dog tightens against her,
and she rubs the plush tuft of neck.
Sometimes, she says, *if I keep my*
eyes shut just like this and try
not to wish it too much, I'll feel your arm
across my pillow, the signal for me
to roll into your body and be held.
So there! And it's all like it was
and you promise to never go away again.
Okay, enough. Wipe your eyes, girl.
Open them. The roses overcome.

Lily bed out of control. Another day. *But I'll lie here one more minute, first. And let you hold me.*

Biographical Note

Gaylord Brewer, a native of Louisville, Kentucky, earned a PhD from Ohio State University. He currently teaches at Middle Tennessee State University, where he founded and for twenty-one years edited the journal *Poems & Plays*. His most recent publication is a cookbook/memoir, *The Poet's Guide to Food, Drink, & Desire* (Stephen F. Austin UP, 2015). He has published 900 poems in journals and anthologies, including *Best American Poetry* and *The Bedford Introduction to Literature*.